Presen...es

Heather Gaston

First published in 1992 by
BELAIR PUBLICATIONS LTD.
P. O. Box 12, Twickenham, England TW1 2QL

Series Editor Robyn Gordon
Series Designer Richard Souper
Photography by Kelvin Freeman
Typesetting by Belair
Printed and Bound by Heanor Gate Printing Limited

ISBN 0 947882 21 9

INTRODUCTION

Children take great pleasure in giving gifts but usually they have a rather limited budget. Any gift, however small or inexpensive, can be made more exciting if it is packaged in an attractive and original way. In this book, I have given a number of ideas for creative ways for children to present an inexpensive gift. Most items would be as suitable for a friend or family member as they would be for a school fair.

These ideas can be adapted to suit a different recipient, or tailored to the skills and particular interests of the child who is giving the present. Most of the ideas are simple and self-explanatory. The most rewarding aspect of designing your own package is to make it as personal as possible for the person who is going to receive it.

All the materials involved are everyday household or classroom materials, or offcuts and snippets of decorative items. These can be saved in the children's homes and brought to school when they have enough to add to the classroom 'pool': useful materials and trimmings from which the ideas in this book, and your own adaptations, can be made.

Many of the items, particularly containers such as mugs, candleholders, glass dishes etc. can be found at charity shops, and a little browsing for the appropriate item can be quite enjoyable. These items are also available at school fetes and jumble sales - it may be worthwhile buying very cheap items to keep for a future venture.

Here is a list of materials used in this book: -
Second-hand china or earthenware cups, mugs, jugs, dishes, plates, bowls, casserole dishes, ash trays, bon-bon dishes, saucers, candleholders, egg cups and ramekins. Glass dishes, drinking glasses, perfume bottles, jam jars, pickling and preserving jars, storage jars and measuring jugs. Paper and card boxes, jewellery boxes, cutlery boxes; books such as novels, children's books, cookery books, sports books etc. Card picture mounts, prints, calendar pictures, postcards. Baskets of all shapes and sizes. Lace and crocheted doilies, trimmings, handkerchiefs and embroidered fabrics. Jewellery: broken necklaces for beads, brooches, earrings etc.

Heather Gaston
1992

CONTENTS

BOXES

Top Row, left: Découpage box covered in scraps from magazines and decorated with gold pen — then varnished. Dried flowers and a ribbon bow are glued on to the lid.

Middle: A cocoa cylinder covered with wrapping paper — the lid has a circle of the paper glued on, then two dried red rose buds and a bow of thin red ribbon glued on to that. The tag is made from a wrapping paper flower glued to red card, cut out and tied with red ribbon.

Right: 'The leopard' box is covered first with white paper (or painted with white emulsion paint). The picture is painted in poster colour and varnished. It can be decorated inside too.

Bottom Row, left: This box in shiny card has the jeweller's name on the lid hidden by a photograph of the giver. It is bordered with a strip of cake wrapper, which also decorates the edge of the box.

Centre: This box is covered with wrapping paper. A fairly dense pattern is essential to hide flaws. A photograph of the recipient's favourite cat is on the lid and it is lined with plain pink art paper.

Right: A wooden camembert box — these are readily available in most supermarkets. This square one has had the cheese labels peeled off and the lid is covered by a section, cut to fit, from a museum postcard. The faded 'papyrus' colours match the box very well.

BOXES

Top Row, left, A heart-shaped cardboard cheese box is covered in heart-shaped magazine scraps in floral prints. The busy pattern hides flaws and joins. It is varnished and decorated with a bow.

Centre: A heart-shaped cheese box is covered with gummed paper. The wreath is made from a circle of small ripped pieces of green gummed paper and tissue, decorated with a bow. The message is in gold pen.

Right: This box is covered in art paper and decorated with ducks cut from white labels and decorated in orange/green pens. The sides have a pattern of poster paint flowers.

Bottom Row, 1st from left: This box has an apple tree design made from overlapping self-adhesive coloured circles (available from stationers). The tree trunk is gummed paper.

2nd: A square camembert box is decorated directly with felt-tip dots.

3rd: The Japanese warrior is from a circular design on a greetings card. It is important to choose suitable shapes. The sides are covered in scraps of decorated patterns from magazines. Gold felt-tip pen is used to pick out the patterns and to border the edge of the lid. It is then varnished.

4th: A cylindrical box had the manufacturer's label printed on it in three places. These labels are covered with paper 'shields' decorated with the recipient's personal heraldic device and initials etc.

Front: This jeweller's box has the brand name covered with pressed leaves and a cut-out paper flower head. The lid is then covered with plastic self-adhesive film.

5

BOXES

Clockwise from bottom left: A Fimo chicken has been made to fit the circular lid of a clear plastic cheese box. The lid has red card fitted to it and then the chicken glued on to that. The chicken is painted with poster paint and varnished.

2nd: This teabag box has the sides covered with gummed paper, each a different colour. There is a collage clown's face on each side drawn on thin card, coloured with pens and appliquéd with wool, bows, silver stars etc.

3rd: This charity shop box is covered with magazine scraps, in shades of blue, turquoise and sea-green. It is decorated with gold pen, gold stars and a gold paper sun. A 'Pisces' motif has been used. The box is decorated inside (see photograph on the title page) continuing the colour and fish theme. The outside of the box is varnished with clear household varnish.

4th: This recycled oval gift box was already covered in floral paper. For a more personal touch, a poem to the recipient has been composed and written on thin green card in an oval shape and glued on to the lid. A bow and silk flowers are glued on the front of the box. Inside the lid there is another card bearing the message.

Centre: This round box has a heart of gummed paper on the lid. There is a border of smaller hearts around the edge of the lid and a wooden Christmas tree toy is glued on the top.

WRAPPINGS

Top: The box is first wrapped in turquoise tissue or art paper and then re-wrapped with greaseproof or tracing paper to produce a semi-translucent glass effect. The design is in silver pen with silver gummed stars and continues in 'waves' all around the package, interspersed with fish, crabs and starfish.

Left: The Tudor portrait is appliquéd on to a gold/red wrapping paper. The face and hands are white card with pen and crayon features and red wool hair, plucked apart to make it curly and fluffy; the body is black gummed paper with gold pen jewellery and a red lentil 'jewel'. The sleeves are purple tissue cut and moulded to shape and stuffed with tissue. The dress embroidery is gold pen, sequins and tiny soup pasta shapes. The cuffs and ruff are scraps of lace and doily. The finger rings are gold pen and lentils. The earrings are tiny seed pearl beads.

Middle: A bar of pink soap is wrapped in a doily, tied at the top with pink ribbon. A tiny white card tie-on tag has a pink heart cut out of the pink ribbon.

Right: The box is wrapped in blue and turquoise tissue and has a silver metal fish (a mould for mousses, available *very inexpensively* at good kitchen shops and department stores). The wave design is in silver pen and the bubbles are silver sequins, some of them glued to green self-adhesive circle stickers (from most stationers).

WRAPPINGS

Top: A large box wrapped in lining wallpaper, with a flower design stencilled on it and the tag. It is tied with red wool and decorated with a bow.

Left: The box is first wrapped in bright pink art paper and then with sections of white doily glued on to fit the shape. This is then wrapped in greaseproof paper and the pattern of the doily picked out in silver pen. A matching tag in pink card with the centre rosette of the doily is attached with pink ribbon.

Centre: This small parcel is wrapped in pink typing paper with a green card Christmas tree glued on with its 'spiked' branches cut and raised for a 3D effect. The decorations include beads, gold/silver pen, 'boxes' of tartan ribbon, unravelled gold braid, gummed stars, tiny beads and silver sequins.

Right: This long parcel is decorated as a street scene. The design of your own street is in coloured pens on white paper. The message says 'with greetings from (your address)'.

WRAPPINGS

Clockwise from left: Stencilled or potato-printed designs can look attractive on plain brown wrapping paper. This simple Christmas tree potato print is decorated with silver pen baubles, garlands and stars. The parcel is tied with red ribbon and a sprig of plastic spruce. The tags are both potato prints: one has a silver pen decoration; the other has sequins.
2nd: The purple parcel is wrapped in white typing paper, painted with purple, pink and blue poster paint circles and blobs. There is a matching ribbon bow.
3rd: The long package (of joss sticks) was suitable for a snake made up from two colours of self-adhesive circles (available from stationers). It is on thin blue card and the message is in black pen.
4th: This parcel is wrapped in white typing paper, with the name 'Lucy' written in two colours of pen in many styles and sizes.
Centre: The tiny parcel is a bathcube (small, flat-shaped soaps work well too) — wrapped in fabric and tied with ric-rac braid. (Small floral prints and thin ribbon fit this idea well.)

WRAPPINGS

Left: The cat package is on white household paper decorated (using coloured felt-tip pens) with a cat design which goes all around the box. Many designs and subjects lend themselves well to this, but especially long animals such as basset hounds, crocodiles, snakes, newts etc. Alternatively, a long, tall person could be drawn lying down. You can applique various parts of the design: this cat has curled ribbon whiskers.

Centre: The sun box design, also on white household paper, is made with potato prints. Each sun's face is then decorated slightly differently with coloured and gold pens. The message 'You are my Sunshine' is in orange pen. It has a sun-shaped tag cut from yellow card.

Right: This is a potato print in yellow paint on dark green tissue paper. Tied on with green ric-rac braid is a circular tag with a cat in green pen.

GLASS JARS AND CONTAINERS

Back Row, left: A jam jar with bath salts has a cover of a pinked circle of tissue tied with ribbon and attached to a small muslin lavender bag. The label has a motif of lavender.

Right: A storage jar, filled with cotton wool, is decorated with suns, moons and stars with silver and gold felt-tip pen. The lid has a gold gummed star and a gold braid bow. The tag is strips of gold foil ribbon on card, cut in a star shape. It is decorated with gold/silver star sequins and gold pen.

Front Row, left to right: A bottle is filled with home-made hand lotion. The label has a rose motif and the tag is a cut-out rose.

2nd: The medicine bottle is covered with hearts of gummed paper.

3rd: The jam-jar, full of home-made bath salts, has a brown paper label and a pinked strip of fabric and the brown paper tag cut in the shape of the word 'Dad'.

4th: The jar is full of shirt buttons. The label is shirt-shaped with blue stripes and a button. The jar's neck has a bright bow-tie.

5th: This jar is filled with bath salts. The flower at the neck is made with tissue petals twisted around a curled ribbon stamen and both tied with more curled ribbon. The tag has a matching flower motif.

GLASS JARS AND CONTAINERS

Top Row, left: A jar filled with sugared almonds, the lid covered in tissue and a doily edged with gold stars and attached with curled ribbon, has 'Mum' written in large letters in gold pen.

Right: This sweet jar, filled with nuts and raisins, is decorated with a gummed paper Christmas tree label and a gummed paper sticker on the lid. The neck is covered with Christmas ribbon.

Middle Row, 1st: A glass goblet, filled with mint imperials, is covered with a sheet of Cellophane tied with long pink ribbon. Flowers are cut out of wrapping paper and appliquéd to the Cellophane.

2nd: A preserving jar, filled with aniseed sweets, has a tie-on label and a cut-out 'sweetie' on the lid.

3rd: This is a glass lemon squeezer filled with lemon sherberts and wrapped in Cellophane. The lemon-shaped card tag is coloured yellow and dotted in green.

Front Row, left: Scottish fudge in a sweet jar has a 'heather' motif, a tiny bow on the label and a tartan ribbon bow at the neck.

Right: This measuring jug is filled with stock cubes and a jar of yeast extract. The tag is cut to the shape of a stockpot.

GLASS JARS WITH MATCHING LID COVERS

Top Row, left: Red peppers, bought in a jar or can, are in a jar with a label decorated with red pen 'peppers'. The gingham lid cover is edged with ric-rac braid and tied with piping cord. A bouquet garni bag in gingham is attached with cord and a wooden bead.

Right: Rose hip jelly is in a jar with a label printed with a 'fingerprint' pink rose. The cover is pinked fabric with a rose design and tied with bias binding.

Middle Row, 1st: Home-made peppermint creams are in a jar with a shamrock label. The cover is floral print (cut from a paper bag) and tied with ribbon. The tag has a shamrock design.

2nd: This jar of marmalade has a label with an 'oranges' design. The lid is covered with a circle of muslin (or net or lace) which has orange beads sewn on at intervals with green thread. (This can be used afterwards as a milk jug cover.)

3rd: Home-made tomato relish is in a jar with a tomato-shaped label. The lid is covered with pinked paper decorated with tomatoes.

Front Row, left: Chilli sauce in a jar with a label decorated with a cut-out 'pepper' and 'DANGER' lettering. The cover is dressmaker's interfacing, tied with ribbon, with a circle of white paper decorated with a ring of red pen 'peppers' around the date.

Right: A pot of honey with a hive-shaped label and coloured with yellow and brown pens. There are two separate cut-out bees. The cover is striped fabric tied with ric-rac braid.

13

EARTHENWARE AND CHINA

Clockwise from bottom left: A small earthenware, casserole-shaped pot holds stock cubes. The matching brown label, tied with string, has an onion design in crayon with the message in pen.

2nd: A chunky, rough-glazed mug from a charity shop is filled with a soap wrapped in brown, rough-textured fabric tied with white piping cord, and contains a wooden shaving brush, two tiny loofah 'face-scrubbers' (these inexpensive items can be bought from most chemists) and a decorative pine cone. The red label in a heart shape is gummed to the mug.

3rd: An old stoneware jar has its cork stopper lined with a circle of pinked brown paper. A brown paper label listing ingredients and decorated with a herb border is glued on. Furnishing cord is tied around the neck and it has a tiny 'shop' label, dyed parchment colour with tea, with the date in pen.

4th: The egg cup is lined with a crocheted doily (charity shops and jumble sales sell these). The chocolate egg is fitted in and decorated with a sprig of artificial flowers.

Centre: A pretty, old-fashioned plate is filled with home-baked cookies protected with cling wrap. The green heart-shaped card has pinked edges and a tiny artificial flower glued on.

EARTHENWARE AND CHINA

Clockwise from bottom left: A giant size mug is filled with shredded tissue and topped with chocolates in silver paper.

2nd: A bowl holds presents for a pet. The bowl is stuffed with tissue and contains a home-made catnip mouse and a bag of cat biscuits. (You could include any suitable items such as a dog comb, pet vitamins, choc drops and chews, collar etc.)

3rd: An egg cup with a rabbit motif contains a chocolate egg wrapped in a tall circle of Cellophane and tied with thin ribbon. The tag is rabbit-shaped, cut from a brown luggage label decorated with pen and a cotton wool 'tail'.

4th: An individual-size oven dish in earthenware used as a holder for an Easter nest made of hay, twisted into a circle which has thin ribbon wound around it. The tiny chocolate eggs are placed in the centre and decorated with a small bow. The tag is a stand-up chick made from yellow card.

5th: A home-made triangular sweet dish (ashtray, soap dish), is filled with shredded Cellophane and contains purple and lilac bath pearls and soap.

6th: The tiny dish is hand-made from Fimo, painted and varnished. It is filled with wooden beads and threading string, then covered in cling film and decorated with a bow.

SUPERMARKET CONTAINERS

Many foods are sold in coloured and clear plastic containers/trays from shops and supermarkets and it seems a good idea to recycle them where possible.

Clockwise from top left: This clear plastic container has the outside edged with white lace and a gathered paper doily inside. The flower-shaped label shows the message written in a circle around a flower centre made from a wooden bead. The cookies are wrapped in Cellophane and then decorated with a bow and tiny 'roses' made from ribbon.

2nd: This shallow tray is lined with crumpled, glued-on tissue and the base is covered with a royal blue 'Fish Curry' recipe card. Three fabric bags of spices are labelled and tied with gold braid and placed in the tray.

Right: Another deep, clear container is filled with macaroon biscuits, each wrapped in tissue covers that have long, fringed, twisted ends and decorated with stars, moons and zig-zags in silver pen.

Centre: A small dessert container in clear plastic is filled with pot-pourri, covered in clear film and decorated with ribbon. The tag is a flower-shaped card with 'stamens' made from seed pearls.

Left, front: A shallow tray is filled with sweet items in cake papers for a gift or a school fête. Decorate the papers with gold/silver pens. Fill with Easter eggs, chocolate coins, petit fours, small biscuits and sweets — tie with curled ribbon.

All sorts of useful or decorative items can be used to contain a gift of sweets, candles etc. and thereby make two gifts in one. Some of the most unlikely items can be combined.

Clockwise from bottom left: A tea-strainer contains an Easter egg and is wrapped in clear film.

2nd: A small bowl contains a candle, a sprinkle of pot-pourri and some bath pearls. It stands on a circle of pinked curtain fabric and is wrapped in a large sheet of Cellophane tied at the top with curled ribbon with a heart-shaped tag attached.

3rd: A heart-shaped baking tin, inexpensively bought from a kitchen shop, is padded with crumpled tissue, and gold chocolate coins are carefully glued in place on top. A loop of blue ribbon is added and there is a blue heart-shaped tag decorated in hearts and marked 'To a Heart of Gold' and attached with gold string.

4th: A pot is filled with pine cones, imitation spruce, red berries and a silver bauble to make a Christmas table decoration.

5th: A wooden spoon contains gold-covered chocolate Easter eggs. The clear film is tied on with gold curled ribbon and there is a tie-on tag in gold pen.

PICTURE FRAMES

A picture is a very welcome present especially if it is a photograph of the giver or another close family member, or a favourite pet, new baby etc. A simple photograph can be made more attractive and personalised if you provide a handmade frame. It is not necessary to go to the expense (and danger) of providing glass at this stage. Second-hand frames can be bought cheaply at jumble sales etc. and (after checking for woodworm) may be renovated, gilded and pictures selected to fit. A painting or a drawing by the giver is also welcome. You can use a card mount which can be bought cheaply from the 'ready made' section in framing shops. Otherwise, a skilled adult must cut one to size. Here are some examples.

Top row: Find a painting, postcard, photograph, to fit the brown card mount and then decorate with gold pen 'stars'. Wrap in Cellophane and add a bow.

Centre: This card has cut-out card flowers glued at one corner decorated in pen. The flower motif is continued in pen along the bottom of the mount around the message 'From .... with love'.

Right: This card has been cut with a roof-shaped top and a design of a family house has been painted around it in watercolour and fine-point black pen. You could make this very personalised, based on your home/their home. It can be made with thin card and even have opening/closing 'doors'.

Front row: These two are made from Fimo modelling clay with varying degrees of modelling ability. They have been painted and varnished.

FLOWER AND PLANT COVERS

Your home-grown plants, herbs, flowers or vegetables make very attractive presents if packaged well. You can also improve shop-bought plants and flowers and make them more personal.

Clockwise from the herb parcel: A pot of mixed herb plants is protected by a square of brown wrapping paper glued on to green thin card, and given a scalloped edge. The brown side has been decorated with sprigs of different herbs each with their name written underneath. Flowing between the sprigs are the words 'From Rebecca's herb garden' in a contrasting colour. The cover is then folded around the pot in a triangular shape. Hole-punch at intervals and tie with narrow ribbon.

Centre: The pink begonia has a wrap-around jacket of pink card edged with zig-zags and holes and decorated with a pleated green tissue paper bow. It has a cut-out 'caterpillar' tag in green.

Right: The rose has a cover of card made from a rectangle wrapped round so that a point is made at the back of the plant. The edge has a row of holes punched and then threaded with thin ribbon.

Centre: The bunch of garden flowers is wrapped in four sheets of zig-zagged tissue — two purple, two turquoise.

Front: The tiny, home-grown wild strawberry has its pot covered with gingham and tied with a red ribbon. It stands on two layers of thin white paper, pinked in circles and bordered with a motif of strawberries.

BOOK COVERS

Homemade, handmade or second-hand books can be inexpensive but made into very attractive and personal gifts.

Left to right: This little dinosaur book is covered in white household paper and decorated with a dinosaur drawn with coloured pens. It is difficult to find ready-coloured paper or card thin enough to cover a book, so often the colouring must be hand done.

2nd: *Black Beauty* is covered in light brown art paper, illustrated in crayon and covered in transparent self-adhesive plastic.

3rd: The hard-backed exercise book is easily converted to an attractive diary or notebook by covering it with richly-patterned wrapping paper and adding two tartan ties, glued on to the inside of each hard cover.

4th: The tiny notebook is a very inexpensive paperback notebook covered in art paper, decorated with dried pressed flowers (glued on) and covered with transparent, self-adhesive plastic.

Centre: An inexpensive, paper-backed exercise book has a cover made from a glued-on postcard cut to size.

BOOK COVERS

Lined and unlined exercise books can be made into very attractive diaries, recipe books, garden diaries, photograph albums, baby progress books, sketch books, notebooks, music notebooks, poetry books etc. depending on the hobby or interest of the recipient. These books can be covered in wrapping paper or your own designed paper. The most effective way is to make a collage cover from magazine cuttings.

Left: 'Jim's Garden Diary' is covered with layers of paper 'leaves' in all shades and sizes. The white title label is overlapped by leaves and bordered by flowers cut from seed packets, magazines etc. You can then add the caterpillar or ladybird made from coloured gummed paper and pens, and glue them on the leaf pattern.

Right: The Jam Recipe Book is made on the same principle from pictures of fruits and blossoms overlapping a lilac-coloured title label made from art paper. The words are in gold and black.

Below: This is an exercise book converted to a Garden Diary by covering it with green art paper, with a deep pocket formed on the inside front cover. This pocket contains packets of seeds. Divide the rest of the exercise book into twelve sections and design a heading for each month. The cover and inside cover of the book can be decorated with designs of vegetables. (The small notebook is described on the previous page.) The dried pressed flower idea looks effective on garden diaries or country sketch books.

BOOK-PLATES

When giving a book, as described on the previous pages, it could be enhanced with your own personalised bookplate for the recipient. If possible, have a look at bookplate designs in old books or a library book on the subject. They were often very beautiful and some were very ingenious in linking the design to the name of the owner of the book. Initials can be linked to make a design; a house-shaped picture of the owner's home; a fruit or flower-shaped plate for a garden book; a fish shape for an angling book; heart shape for a romance. You can use a play on the name, if possible, with a picture of a fisher, a tailor, a thatcher, a cook, a smith, a robin, an (ingot of) gold, a pool, (Walters, Lake, River). The bookplate shown glued on the red-leafed book has an initial design in a petit-point style. Here are a few more examples:-

Left to right: Yacht shape for a book on ships; a cat sitting on stack of books; a black/white circular plate with a design of a fisherman for 'Paul Fisher'. A jar-shaped plate with a gingham lid-cover for a cookbook; a window and window box view which could be copied from the recipient's own house and curtains. Black and white bookplate designs can be photocopied, so that you can give several, in a packet, to one person as a gift in itself. These can be left in monochrome or coloured individually.

BOOKMARKS

As mentioned previously, when giving books there are various ways to make the gift more attractive. One way is to provide a bookmark to accompany the book. In such an instance, the bookmark could be designed to complement the book, i.e. bears for *Winnie the Pooh*, yachts for *Swallows and Amazons*, ghostly shapes for a ghost story etc. If you have made and illustrated the book yourself, then it would be even more satisfying to add a matching bookmark. Bookmarks can be made out of anything that is flat, so paper and ribbon are the usual choice. Here are a few ideas.

Left to right: A pattern of dried flowers glued lightly to a strip of dark blue card and covered with clear, self-adhesive plastic.

2nd: This card bookmark is decorated with a child's fingerprints converted to 'beetles and bugs' with black pen.

3rd: This mark is a strip of ric-rac braid and a strip of white piping cord glued on to a narrow strip of red card.

4th: This is simply lengths of embroidery wool, plaited, with a white tie-on label.

5th: An elephant brooch, which can be bought or made from Fimo, card, bread dough etc., is pinned on to a length of matching card and the message written in coloured pen.

6th: Tall, thin designs like kites and balloons are very suitable: the bear and the balloon are of coloured paper glued on strong card. The balloon 'string' is thin ribbon. There is a reading motto in coloured pen.

TAGS

It is best to make the hole for the tie string with a hole punch. This will look neater than using scissors and is less dangerous.

Top Row, left to right: A folded bear-shaped tag with blue card bow-tie and feet.

Middle: A long card can be made to fit a long shape like this basset hound which is a pun on the recipient's name.

Right: A candle-shaped card covered in coloured gummed paper suitable for Christmas or Divali, with gold string.

Middle Row: A bear shape, cut on folded paper, with a ribbon bow-tie.

Middle: A glove-shaped card with paper doily and ribbon 'cuff'.

Right: A photocopied view of your town, taken from a guide book, postcard etc. and glued to green card and partially 'tinted' with watercolour or coloured pen. Add 'Greetings from.............' in pen.

Bottom Row: Choose a flower or similar motif from a patterned fabric. Glue on to a piece of coloured card. Cut around the shape of the flower and punch a hole for the tie (bias binding).

Middle: The same process as for the previous tag but using wallpaper.

Right: A brown card luggage label with the message in two colours of felt-tip pen and border design around the hole.

Front: A design on dark blue card, made from pellets of coloured silver foil; they are arranged as a flower with gold stem and gold paper leaves.

TAGS

Top Row: left: It is a nice idea to personalise a design around the name of the recipient, as in this simple folded card with a sea shell design for 'Michelle' and **right:** A windmill design on a brown luggage label for 'Jodie Miller'.

Middle Row: A Christmas wreath made from twisting very thin birch twigs into a circle and attaching the ends with fine wire or string, and then looping thin satin ribbon around to hold it together. (You could use hay or straw for this.) The wreath is decorated with a bow, pinked leaves and red berries made from self-adhesive circular labels.

Middle and right: The next three tags are all cut-outs of the recipient's name treated in different ways. 'Susie' is plain pink card and thin ribbon; 'Yuri' has the name repeated all over it in coloured pen in two colours; 'Vijay' is written as two initials interlocking and coloured in felt-tip pen.

Front Row: A photograph of the giver is glued on to a circle of card and there is a matching loop of ric-rac braid.

Centre: An oval of dark blue card with dried flowers glued on is covered in transparent, self-adhesive plastic and has a tiny bow.

Right: A teapot shape has been cut from a magazine photograph of a blue-white floral plate and glued to thin card. The hole is punched through the teapot handle and a gingham ribbon attached.

BASKETS

There are many baskets to be found in cupboards, sales, charity shops etc. Just fit a suitable basket to your gift and decorate it.

Clockwise from the top: This basket holds a gift of tangerines. The basket is lined with a rectangle of dark green tissue with edges cut in long points and then re-lined with white (or coloured) net fabric cut in the same way. The tangerine-shaped tag is in orange and green card.

2nd: The little blue basket has a fabric bow glued on the front and then the whole basket and bow is painted over with a coat of white emulsion (under supervision). When dry, a second coat of emulsion, with a little blue poster paint added, is applied and allowed to dry. The basket is lined with paper doily. Shell-shaped soaps, wrapped in Cellophane, are put inside.

3rd: A shallow basket with handles is lined with a rectangle of pinked, candy-striped fabric. The soap has a personalised label with the giver's name and flower sprigs. A row of bath pearls is added and a bow tied to each handle of the basket.

4th: The swan-shaped basket is filled with small soaps wrapped in Cellophane. A ribbon around the swan's neck holds a swan-shaped tag.

5th: This tiny basket holds four or five wooden scented 'pears' with a border of green leaves decorated with dark green pen.

CANDLES

Candles should be made with adult supervision. The wax can be collected from left-over pieces of candles or wax pellets can be bought from craft shops. Aromatic oils can be added to make scented candles: follow the instructions from the shop for this.

Left: A china bowl is lined with a circle of purple tissue and a ring of green tissue paper leaves, then filled with tiny candles made in petit four patty tins, decorated with artificial flowers.

Top: Two beeswax candles are tied together with ribbon.

Top Right: A supermarket plastic dessert bowl filled with water holds two floating candles.

Centre: A nightlight and a sherry glass are decorated with gold hearts. A red ribbon is tied around the glass stem.

Bottom Row, left to right: A liqueur glass is filled with wax and a wick, wrapped in a curve of paper doily, then tied with a ribbon. It has a candle-shaped tag saying 'Happy Divali'.

2nd: A shallow glass dish, filled with wax, is trimmed with a plastic bracelet and wrapped in clear film.

3rd: The china ashtray holds a Christmas arrangement that includes a green candle made in a cake paper mould (use three or four papers), fabric 'holly' leaves, silver plastic berries and a silver paper parcel. The tag is tartan ribbon glued to card.

Right: A tiny bowl contains a nightlight candle; it is wrapped in Cellophane and tied with ribbon.

ENVELOPES

Envelopes can be decorated with messages and designs to please the recipient or to fit the occasion. You can make stickers from self-adhesive labels, cut to shape. You can design your own stamps and attach them.

Top Row, left to right: A honey-coloured envelope has a cut-out bee for a sticker and rows of tiny bees in crayon.

2nd: Gold pen messages look good on rich dark colours.

3rd: The 'V' shape has been adapted to a hawk's head with crayon.

2nd Row: A sky-blue envelope, suitable for airmail, has a cut-out cloud for a sticker. A plane is drawn on and the message written on the cloud.

2nd: The pink envelope shows a postman cut from a wrapping paper design, with his footprints in black pen.

3rd: The 'V' shape has been adapted to a cat's face in crayon.

4th: The bright pink envelope says 'To my fabulous Mummy' and has a blue card Egyptian mummy's head decorated in black and gold.

Third Row: The bright green card is delivered by hand and has a pink card cut-out hand on the front with a rolled-up gold paper ring.

2nd: This bright pink envelope has a Christmas tree sticker made of green and red gummed paper, decorated with silver pen and a silver star.

3rd: This blue envelope has a stamp design on it featuring the giver's mother as a queen drawn in coloured and gold pen, and the rest of the envelope decorated with national symbols and flags to reinforce the message of the 'best mother in the world'.

CARDS WITH A TINY GIFT

Back Row: A simple fold green card has an appliquéd hand in pink card glued on to the front. The cuff is paper doily and ribbon, and the rings gold paper and a lentil. The fingernails and message are in pink pen and a covered teabag fits behind the hand. Details of 'time to come to tea' etc. are on the inside.

2nd: A simple fold card is made of two rectangles of one green, one yellow card glued together with the edges pinked. The card is then folded so that a border of yellow shows. The brooch, which can be home-made, is pinned on to the front of the card and the message written in coloured pen. Pen 'paw prints' make a pattern on the yellow border. It is decorated with thin green ribbon.

Front Row: A simple fold card in pale green card has a pink elephant hair ornament clipped on and the accompanying palm tree and message in coloured pen.

4th: Another simple fold card in pink has a jumble sale brooch, around which the card is designed and decorated.

CARDS WITH A TINY GIFT

Top to bottom: A royal blue simple fold card has gummed paper strips in gold and purple to form medal ribbons. The 'medal' is a gold foil-covered chocolate coin and the message in gold pen says 'To a Dad who deserves a medal'.

2nd: A simple fold white card has a face of your friend drawn in coloured pen; the gift of earrings is pinned on the ear lobes.

3rd: A rectangle of stiff white card has a collage picture of an alligator (made from magazine cuttings) with his jaws open showing a row of white card teeth made with pinking shears. The card is cut along the line of the jaw and a tiny gift, wrapped in tissue and ribbon (e.g. could be a small chocolate bar, chewing gum etc.) is fitted in. The placatory message says 'Sorry I snapped at you'.

4th: A simple fold white card has a heart-shaped design that contains a tiny white lace bag filled with small pink sweets and glued on firmly. The bag has a pink ribbon bow and the rest of the card is filled in and decorated with pink/orange pens. The message says 'Sweets for my Sweet'.

FOLDERS

Folders can be made to enhance all sorts of gifts, provided the gift is reasonably flat. Cards, postcards, photographs, notelets, writing paper and envelopes, stamps etc. are eminently suitable. A combination folder of writing materials and stamps can be made as in the photograph (see above), the cover and insides decorated with designs in pen, watercolour, crayon etc. Other items that could be considered are seed packets (see photograph above); a First Aid folder of gauze and adhesive plasters; a 'New Baby' folder of cotton buds and a face cloth; a 'body' folder of soap leaves, packets of bath salts, sachets of lotion etc.; a cookery collection of recipe cards, bookmark, packet of saffron; a tea folder with sachets of different flavour teas etc.

SUGGESTIONS FOR GIFTS

A great many of these items can be homemade, which will make them more personal and possibly less expensive. If bought from shops, none of these suggestions are outside the average budget for a child and many are obtainable from charity shops and school fêtes.

Jewellery, buttons, small sewing kits, embroidery silks and wools, hair ornaments and ties, neckties, bow ties, tie clips, gloves and mittens, scarves.

Sweets, candies, chewing gum, Easter eggs, chocolate coins, nuts, dried fruit, crystallised fruit.

Jams, jellies, marmalade, honey, preserved fruit and vegetables, mustard, pickles, sauces, herbs, cookies, cakes, pastries, stock cubes, bouquet garni bags, vinegars, spices, tea bags, fresh fruit and vegetables.

Soaps, bath salts, bath pearls, bath cubes, emery boards, loofah offcuts, sponges, combs, powder puff, shaving brush, lavender bags, pot-pourri, face and body lotion, shampoo, hair conditioner, aftershave, cologne, cotton wool, cleaning pads and other small cosmetic items.

Pens, pencils, crayons, paintbrushes, paints, paper, writing paper, envelopes, stamps, notebooks, exercise books, sketchbooks, paper clips, elastic bands, drawing pins (tacks), pen holders, pencil sharpeners, erasers, key ring, ruler.

Reading books, diaries, bookmarks, book-plates, recipe books and cards, address books, birthday books, visitors' books, baby books, photograph albums, scrapbooks, jigsaws, puzzles, boxed games, glass marbles, soft toys.

Oven mitts, chopping board, lemon squeezer, wooden spoons and other small, useful kitchen items, table napkins and holders, candles, joss sticks.

Paintings, drawings, self portraits, silhouettes, collages, dried flower pictures, samplers, embroidered pictures, postcards, prints, calendars.

Flowers, plants, herb plants, cuttings, table decorations, dried flower arrangements, seeds, plant food, window box-sized trowel, garden gloves, string, bird feeders, bird boxes, bird seed, pet food and pet toys.